Leonardo
The greatest ~~~ who ever lived?

written by Herbie Brennan
illustrated by Lee Montgomery

Leonardo's early life	2
Leonardo learns to paint	4
Leonardo and the Duke of Milan	6
Inventions	8
Making maps for the Borgias	18
The *Mona Lisa*	19
Leonardo's final years	20
Leonardo's life – a map	21
Timeline	22
Index	24

Leonardo's early life

Many people believed that Leonardo da Vinci was the greatest genius who ever lived. Read on to see if you agree!

Leonardo was born on 15 April, 1452, in the little town of Vinci, not far from Florence in Italy. (His name actually means "Leonardo from Vinci.")

His father worked as a notary (someone who prepares legal papers). His mother was a poor country woman.

Leonardo invented a special kind of backward writing. You have to use a mirror to read it. He might have used mirror writing to make it harder for people to read his notes and steal his ideas.

This is an example of mirror writing. Can you work out what it says?

Leonardo learns to paint

When he was about fourteen, Leonardo went to learn painting from a master painter called Verrocchio. He learned how to make paint and how to get surfaces ready to be painted on. He tried to invent new ways of making paint and preparing surfaces. This did not always work. Some of his paintings cracked, peeled and faded with time.

But by the time he was 20 years old, Leonardo was a better painter than Verrocchio. In this picture by Verrocchio, Leonardo painted the more beautiful angel, on the left, with long, curly hair.

Leonardo and the Duke of Milan

Painters in the fifteenth century couldn't sell their pictures in galleries the way artists do today. Leonardo had to find someone rich who would pay him to paint pictures. These rich people were called patrons.

Portrait of the Duke of Milan

Leonardo's first patron was the Duke of Milan. He was so impressed by Leonardo's paintings that he employed him for nearly eighteen years.

As well as studying art, Leonardo also studied maths, physics and biology.

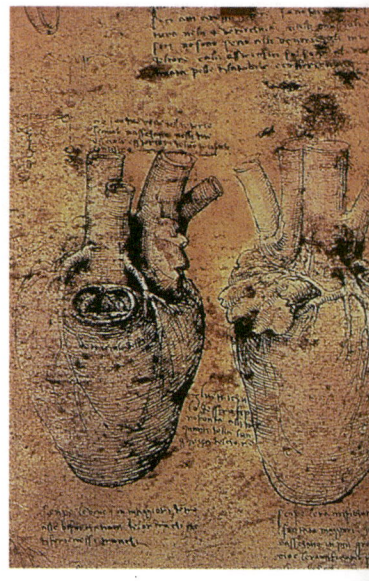

He was fascinated by the way the human body worked. He sketched muscles and sinews again and again. The more he sketched, the better he became at painting.

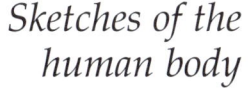

Sketches of the human body

The Madonna of the Rocks

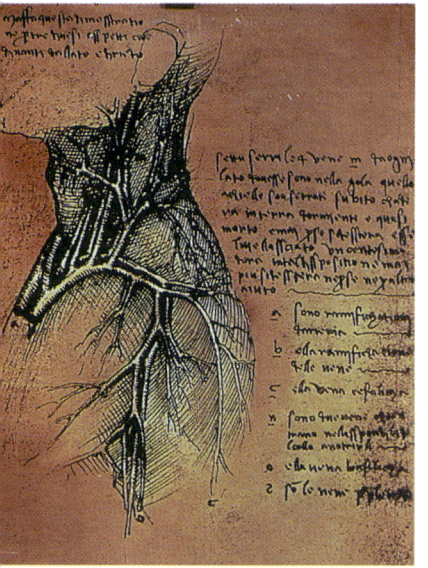

Leonardo only finished six paintings during the eighteen years he worked for the Duke of Milan. But some of these paintings became very famous, for example *The Madonna of the Rocks* and *The Last Supper*.

Inventions

While he was working for the Duke of Milan, Leonardo also invented some amazing things. He worked on plans for:

a camera	axles	pistons
screws	gears	a pump
keys	brakes	springs

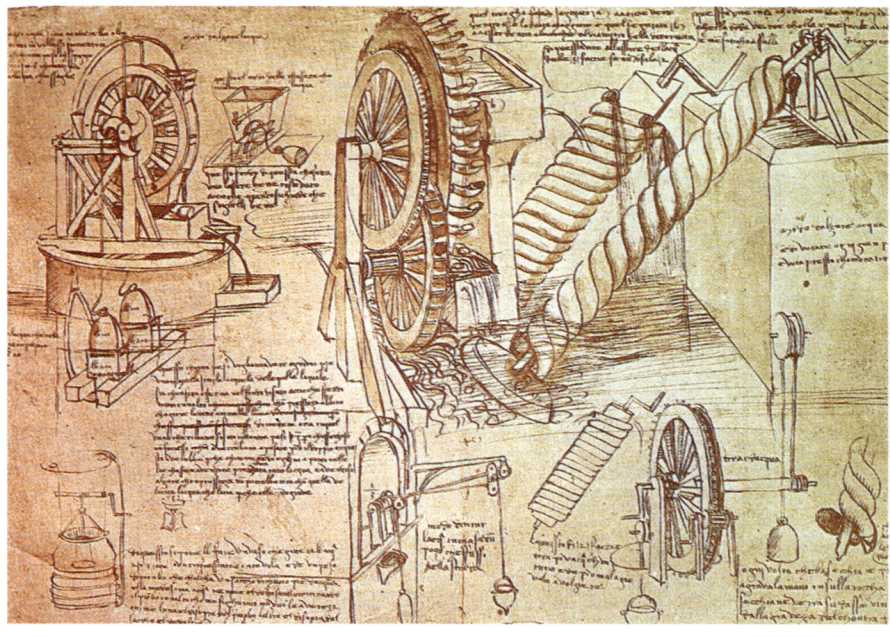

He made drawings for an invention to lift a steady supply of water from streams.

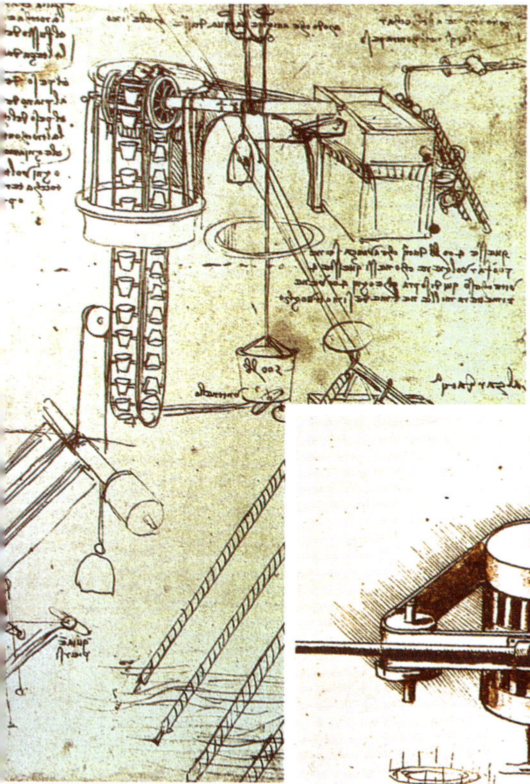

Plans for a water wheel with cups.

A sketch for a spinning machine.

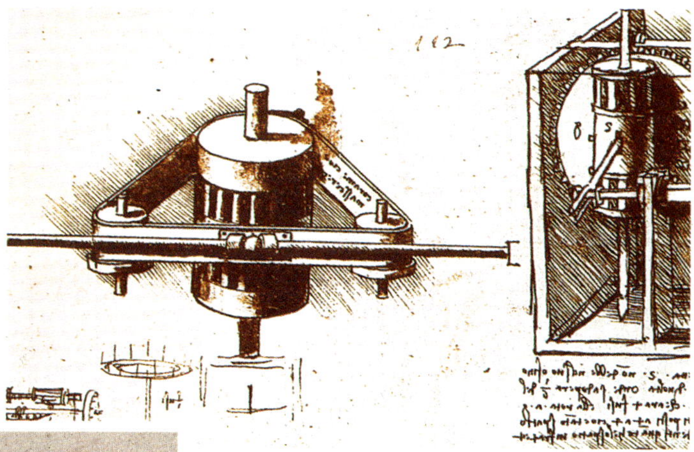

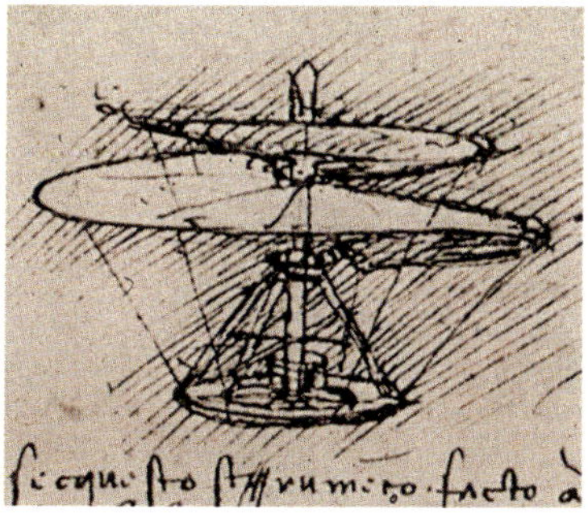

Leonardo even drew plans for a helicopter!

People often think these things were invented hundreds of years after Leonardo died.

Musical instruments

Leonardo was interested in music and invented many musical instruments. He invented a flute that sounded like a human voice and a drum that played by itself.

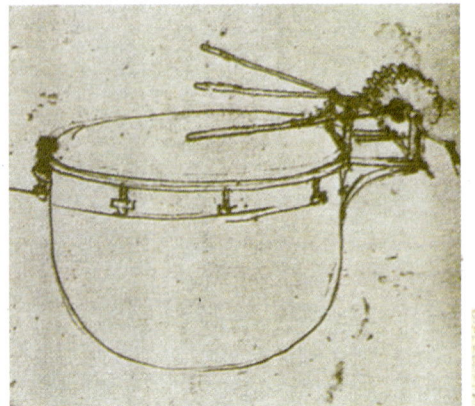

A mechanical drum

He even sketched a bagpipe costume, which allowed musicians to play the bagpipes while riding a horse.

Leonardo played several instruments, including the lute.

Weapons

Leonardo's patron, the Duke of Milan, often went to war. So even though he hated war, Leonardo also invented a great many weapons.

A tank

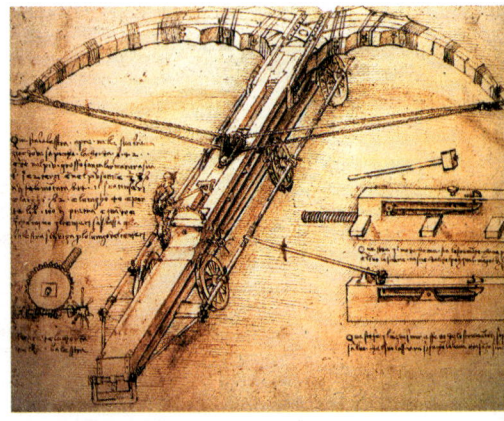

A crossbow

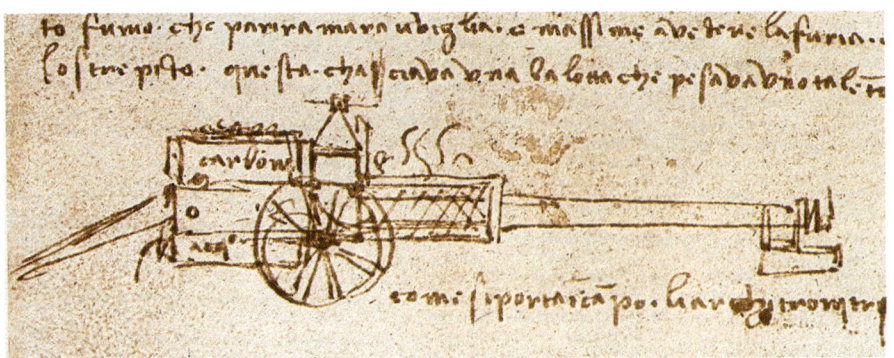

A steam-powered cannon

Warships

Leonardo invented two warships. One has a 'scorpion' arm and the other a moveable ram.

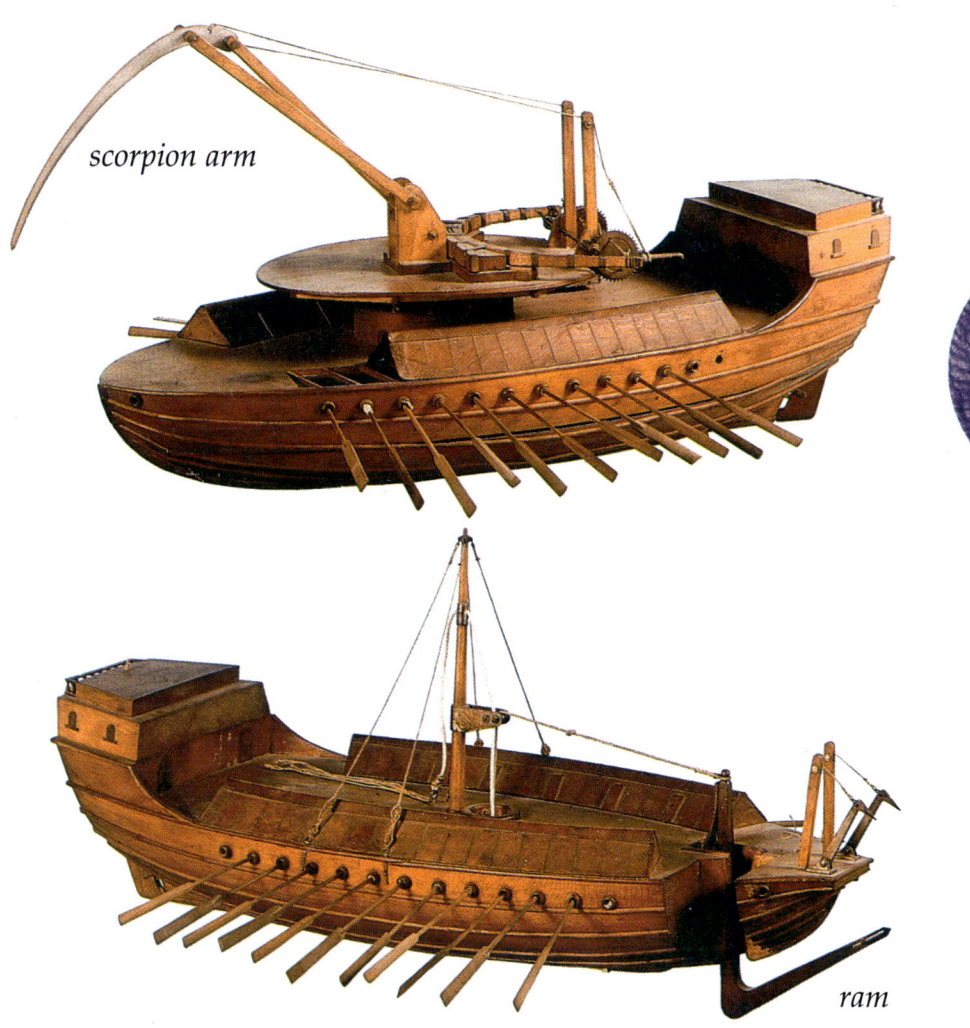

scorpion arm

ram

An aeroplane

Leonardo created his most amazing designs when he tried to invent an aeroplane.

A model made from Leonardo's aeroplane designs.

He thought that an aeroplane could fly in the same way that a bird does, with wings that flap up and down to keep it in the air.

A parachute

He also designed a parachute that works!

Leonardo's parachute really works!

In July 2000, a British man named Adrian Nicholas tested it. He jumped from a plane and used a parachute made from Leonardo's design to get safely down to earth.

Leonardo's design for a parachute

A bicycle

One of Leonardo's most surprising inventions was the bicycle. More than any other, this invention shows how very clever Leonardo was.

There were no bicycles at all in Leonardo's time. And even when people began to use bicycles hundreds of years later, they were less advanced than the one he invented.

A model made from Leonardo's sketch of a bicycle.

The penny-farthing bicycle was invented in the 1800s. It had no gears, no chain, and people found it very difficult to ride without falling off!

Leonardo's design was made nearly four hundred years before the penny-farthing was invented. It shows a bicycle with two wheels the same size, and pedals that drove the back wheels by means of a chain. In fact it was very much like the bicycles people ride today.

Making maps for the Borgias

Leonardo's job in Milan came to an end when the Duke lost a war with the French. Leonardo then had to leave Milan.

He found a new job making maps for one of Italy's most important families, the Borgias.

The Borgias had a habit of poisoning people they didn't like, but they must have liked Leonardo! He survived and returned to Florence in 1503.

One of Leonardo's military maps

The *Mona Lisa*

It was in Florence that he painted one of the world's most famous paintings, the *Mona Lisa*.

For centuries, people have wondered who she is, and why she is smiling in this mysterious way.

Mona Lisa

Leonardo's final years

In 1516, Leonardo left Italy to advise the King of France on building design. He died on 2 May, 1519. He was 67 years old.

When you think of all Leonardo's inventions, his great paintings, and how he studied everything from musical instruments to the way muscles work, you can see he was a genius – perhaps the greatest genius who ever lived. Do you agree?

Leonardo da Vinci: born 1452, died 1519

Leonardo's life – a map

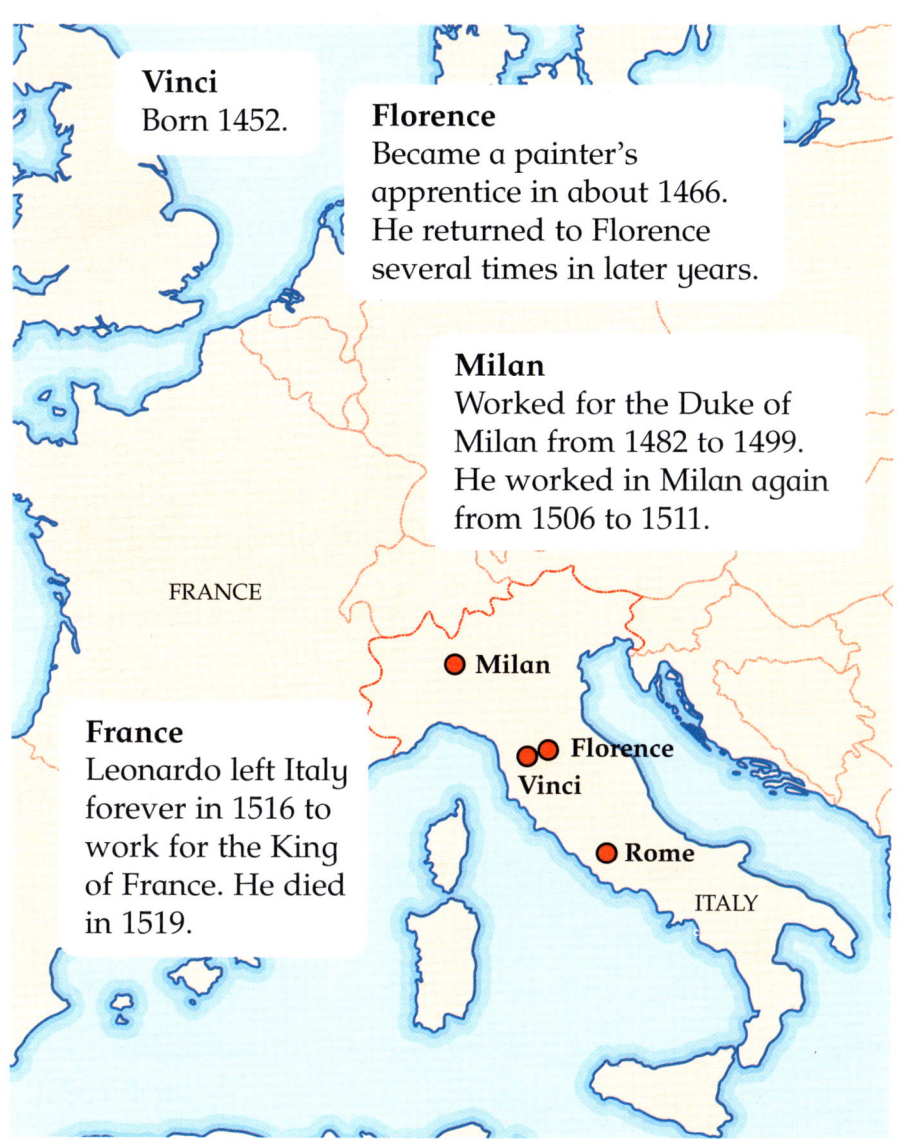

Vinci
Born 1452.

Florence
Became a painter's apprentice in about 1466. He returned to Florence several times in later years.

Milan
Worked for the Duke of Milan from 1482 to 1499. He worked in Milan again from 1506 to 1511.

France
Leonardo left Italy forever in 1516 to work for the King of France. He died in 1519.

Timeline

Moves to Florence and learns to paint.

Begins to work for the Duke of Milan.

1466   1481

1452   1476

Born in Vinci.   Has his own
                        artists' workshop.

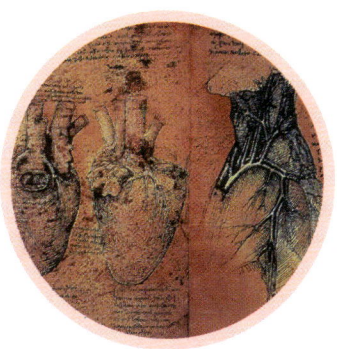

Moves to Milan. Leonardo studies machines and the human body.

Leaves Italy to work for the King of France.

1506   1516

1503   1514   1519

Paints the Mona Lisa while living in Florence.

Lives in Rome.

Dies in France, aged 67, on 2 May.

Index

aeroplane   14

bicycle   16–17
biology   6
Borgias   18

drawings and sketches   7, 8, 9, 10, 12, 15, 16, 17

Florence   2, 18, 19
France, King of   20

human body   7

Last Supper, The   7

Madonna of the Rocks, The   7
maps   18
maths   6
Milan, Duke of   6–7, 8, 12, 18
Mona Lisa   18
musical instruments   10–11, 20

painting   4–5, 7, 19, 20
parachute   15
patron   6, 12
penny-farthing   17
physics   6

Vinci   2

war   12, 13
weapons   12
writing   3